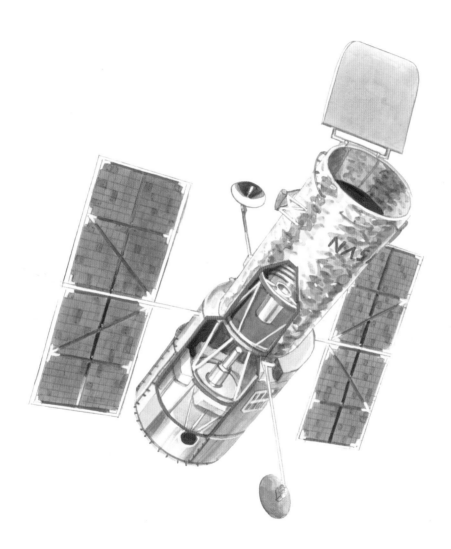

A Satellite Timeline

1957

The Soviet Union launches the first satellite, Sputnik 1. Later the same year, Sputnik 2 carries a dog called Laika into orbit.

1961

Soviet pilot Yuri Gagarin becomes the first human satellite when he makes one orbit of Earth in his Vostok 1 capsule.

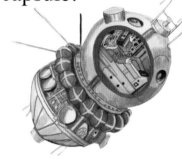

1959

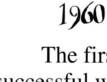

Explorer 6 sends back the first photographs of Earth taken by a satellite.

1958

Explorer 1, the first US satellite, discovers radiation belts around Earth.

1960

The first successful weather satellite, TIROS 1, is launched.

1971

The Soviet Union launches the first space station, Salyut 1.

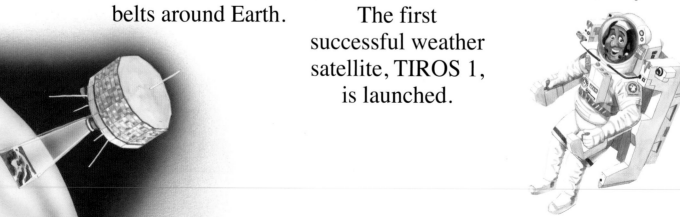

1981

The first Space Shuttle, *Columbia*, is launched into Earth orbit.

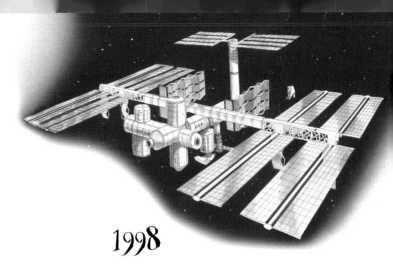

1998

Construction of the International Space Station begins in Earth orbit.

1978

The first global positioning satellite, Navstar 1, is launched.

2013

STRaND 1, the first satellite operated by the computer in a smartphone, is launched.

1990

The Hubble Space Telescope is launched.

Satellite Launch Sites

1. Baikonur Cosmodrome (Russia)
2. Cape Canaveral (USA)
3. Jiuquan (China)
4. Kagoshima (Japan)
5. Kennedy Space Center (USA)
6. Kourou (European Space Agency, South America)
7. Pacific Spaceport (USA) (formerly known as the Kodiak Launch Complex)
8. Palmachim (Israel)
9. Plesetsk Cosmodrome (Russia)
10. Satish Dhawan Space Centre (India) (formerly Sriharikota)
11. Taiyuan (China)
12. Tanegashima (Japan)
13. Vandenberg AFB (USA)
14. Wallops Flight Facility (USA) (formerly Wallops Island)
15. Xichang (China)
16. Vostochny Cosmodrome (Russia) (formerly Svobodny)
17. Yasny (Russia)

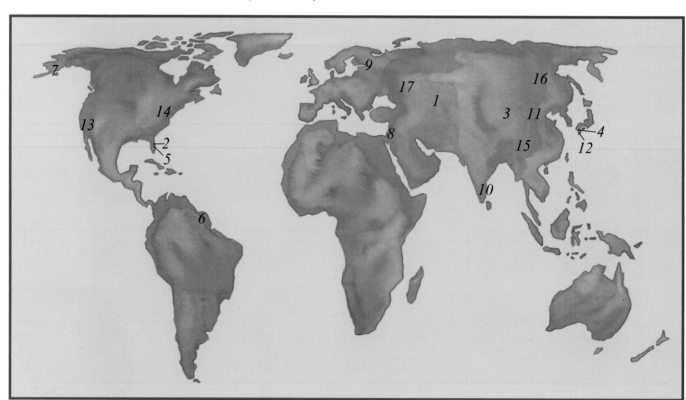

Author:

Ian Graham earned a degree in applied physics at City University, London. He then earned a degree in journalism. Since becoming a freelance author and journalist, he has written more than 250 children's nonfiction books.

Artist:

Mark Bergin was born in Hastings, England, in 1961. He studied at Eastbourne College of Art and specializes in historical reconstructions, aviation, and maritime subjects. He lives in Bexhill-on-Sea with his wife and children.

Editor: **Jonathan Ingoldby**

Editorial Assistant: **Isobel Lundie**

PAPER FROM SUSTAINABLE FORESTS

Published in Great Britain in 2019 by
The Salariya Book Company Ltd
25 Marlborough Place, Brighton BN1 1UB

Library of Congress Cataloging-in-Publication Data
Names: Graham, Ian, 1953- author.
Title: You wouldn't want to live without satellites! / written by Ian Graham ; illustrated by Mark Bergin.
Description: Brighton ; New York : Franklin Watts, an Imprint of Scholastic Inc., 2019. | Series: You wouldn't want to live without | Includes index.
Identifiers: LCCN 2018003411| ISBN 9780531128169 (library binding) | ISBN 9780531193648 (pbk.)
Subjects: LCSH: Artificial satellites--Juvenile literature.
Classification: LCC TL796.3 .G73 2019 | DDC 629.46--dc23 LC record available at https://lccn.loc.gov/2018003411

All rights reserved.
Published in 2019 in the United States
by Franklin Watts
An imprint of Scholastic Inc.

Printed and bound in China.
Printed on paper from sustainable sources.
1 2 3 4 5 6 7 8 9 10 R 28 27 26 25 24 23 22 21 20 19

You Wouldn't Want to Live Without™
Satellites!

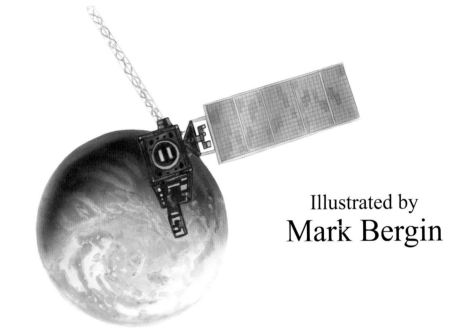

Written by
Ian Graham

Illustrated by
Mark Bergin

Franklin Watts®
An Imprint of Scholastic Inc.

Contents

Introduction

The Space Age began with the launch of the first satellite, Sputnik 1, in 1957. It was a simple metal ball with radio transmitters inside, but it began a revolution in science and technology that continues today.

A satellite is a small object traveling around something bigger. The Moon is a natural satellite of Earth. A spacecraft launched into orbit around Earth is an artificial satellite. Since Sputnik 1, about 6,000 more satellites have been launched by 40 countries. Nearly 4,000 are still in orbit, and more than 1,700 of them are still working.

You use satellites every day without knowing it. They relay telephone calls, television pictures, and Internet messages around the world. Weather forecasts and navigation rely on satellites, too. And lots of businesses depend on satellites. They're so important for so many of the things we do every day that you wouldn't want to live without satellites.

The First Satellites

The idea that something could be made to orbit the Earth is hundreds of years old, but it wasn't possible until the development of powerful rockets during the 20th century. A satellite orbiting near Earth has to reach a speed of about 17,000 miles per hour (28,000 kilometers per hour). When the Soviet Union launched the first satellite, Sputnik 1, in 1957, it stunned the world. Their next satellite, Sputnik 2, carried the first living creature into space, a dog called Laika. Other countries, especially the United States, were quick to catch up and launch their own satellites.

There it is!

SPUTNIK 1 ORBITED EARTH every 96 minutes. The radio bleeps it transmitted could be picked up by all the countries it passed over.

N.A.S.A.

It's the biggest ball I've ever seen!

How It Works

Some satellites orbit the Earth from pole to pole, but most orbit Earth's equator. A satellite 22,000 miles (36,000 km) above the equator stays above the same spot on the ground. It's called geostationary orbit.

Polar orbit

Geostationary orbit

A SATELLITE CALLED ECHO 1, launched in 1960, was a metal-coated balloon 100 feet (30 meters) across. Radio signals sent up to it bounced back down to Earth. It showed that satellites could be used for radio communication.

IN 1962, TELSTAR 1 was the first satellite to relay television pictures across the Atlantic Ocean. It was famous. A record called *Telstar*, named after the satellite, reached Number 1 on the music charts.

THE FIRST SATELLITES were launched by governments and their space agencies, but Intelsat 1 was different. Nicknamed Early Bird, in 1965 it was the first satellite launched by NASA but built for a private business.

Watching Earth

Satellites watch Earth for all sorts of reasons. Apart from weather forecasting, they take pictures of forest fires, floods, and other natural disasters. They study sea ice and glaciers. They see where forests are being cleared. They can even spot diseases and growth problems in farm crops and forests. Many of these things are easier to see from space than on the ground, because satellites look down on large areas of the Earth's surface. If there were no satellites, this work would be more difficult and some of it might not be done at all.

WHEN OIL IS SPILLED by a ship or drilling rig at sea, aircraft and satellites watch where it goes and warn if it floats toward a coastline.

CLIMATE SCIENTISTS want to know how much ice there is at the North and South Poles and in glaciers, and whether the ice is growing or shrinking. Satellites provide this information.

Where'd the ice go?

The satellite was right!

At the surface

Satellite images show new details

Maps drawn from the images reveal houses

You Can Do It!

You can see how satellites orbit Earth by scrunching paper into a ball and sticking it to a piece of string with sticky tape. Whirl it around your head. The string pulls the ball into a circular path, just like gravity pulling a satellite into an orbit.

ARCHAEOLOGISTS use satellites to search for ancient settlements. The marks left in the ground by such buildings are often invisible at ground level, but show up clearly from space.

Visible light   *Infrared*

SATELLITES CAN SEE Earth in ways that we can't. They can take infrared (heat) pictures. The different colors in these images of a hurricane show different temperatures, revealing extra information.

Will It Rain?

All sorts of everyday activities depend on knowing what the weather will be like. Will you need to wear a coat when you go out? Will snow close airports? Will it be too wet for farmers to harvest their crops? Will it be stormy at sea? Weather forecasters used to rely on reports from ships, aircraft, and weather stations on land. They had to piece together these reports to get a picture of the weather. Today, satellites let forecasters see weather systems forming over the oceans, mountains, and deserts where there are few weather stations, making weather forecasts more accurate.

THE FIRST SUCCESSFUL weather satellite, TIROS 1, was launched on April 1, 1960. Its job was to find out if satellites would be useful for studying the Earth.

WEATHER FORECASTS are more reliable now than ever before thanks to photographs of the Earth and its swirling, cloudy atmosphere, taken by weather satellites.

See how good a weather forecaster you are. Look at the sky. The clouds show which way the wind is blowing. Is better weather on the way? Write down your forecast for tomorrow. Were you right?

WEATHER SATELLITES can spot dangerous storms when they are still far away from land. People in their path can be warned so that they can be prepared, take cover, or leave the area.

GOES 16 is one of many US weather satellites circling the Earth. It was launched in 2016. Many other countries also have weather satellites.

11

Communications Satellites

R adio signals usually travel in straight lines. Most radio signals don't follow the curved shape of the Earth's surface. One way to send messages to people beyond the horizon is to lay communication cables all over the world. Another way is to use satellites. Communications satellites can relay telephone calls to and from remote places where there are no telephone lines on the ground. Ships and aircraft often use satellite phones, too. Satellites can also link remote places to the Internet. If there were no satellites, long-distance communication would be more difficult.

SATELLITE TELEPHONES work in places where no other phone would get a signal. They let explorers, sailors at sea, and aid workers in remote places keep in touch with the rest of the world.

Yes, Mom, I am getting enough to eat!

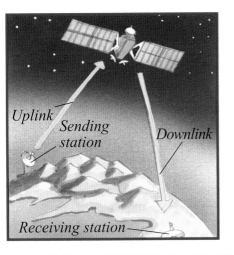

Uplink
Sending station
Downlink
Receiving station

COMMUNICATIONS SATELLITES "see" so far because they are so high above the ground. The radio signal sent up to them is called the uplink and the signal that comes down is the downlink.

You Can Do It!

Make a yogurt-carton phone. Make a small hole in the bottom of two empty yogurt cartons. Thread the ends of a long piece of string through the holes and tie knots. Hold the cartons so that the string is tight, and have a chat.

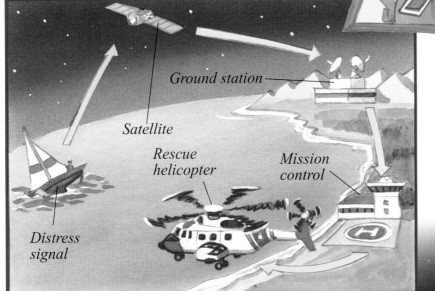

Ground station
Satellite
Rescue helicopter
Mission control
Distress signal

EMERGENCY RADIO BEACONS send distress signals that are picked up by satellites and relayed to the nearest search-and-rescue services.

A FLEET OF IRIDIUM SATELLITES provides worldwide satellite phone services. Sixty-six of these satellites orbit Earth 483 miles (777 km) above the ground.

Where Am I?

The satellites of the Global Positioning System (GPS) can tell you precisely where you are, anywhere in the world. They orbit Earth at a height of 12,500 miles (20,200 km). A GPS receiver picks up radio signals from the satellites and uses them to figure out how far it is from them. It needs signals from at least four satellites in order to do this. GPS started out as a military system, but now anyone can use it. It makes travel and transportation quicker, easier, and safer, because sailors, pilots, and travelers need never get lost.

A SWARM OF 27 GPS satellites surrounds the Earth. They're spaced out so that at least six satellites are always in view from anywhere on Earth.

You have reached your destination.

Are we there yet?

A GPS UNIT in a car uses radio signals from GPS satellites to figure out the car's position and then displays it on a digital road map.

THE GLOBAL POSITIONING
SYSTEM was created so that US
Navy submarines could figure out
exactly where they were if they
surfaced in the middle of a vast
ocean.

We're at
14.59°S, 28.67°W

THANKS TO SATELLITES, the
positions of ships are now known
with great precision. This means
that fewer ships run into rocks,
reefs, and shores as a result of a
ship not being exactly where the
crew thinks it is.

Astronauts in Orbit

Wow! That's the International Space Station.

Orbiting spacecraft carrying people are satellites, too. More than 300 spacecraft carrying people have been launched since the first, Vostok 1, took Soviet pilot Yuri Gagarin into orbit in 1961. Since the US Space Shuttle stopped flying in 2011, only Russia and China have been able to launch crewed spacecraft into orbit, but at least 10 new crewed spacecraft are being developed by space agencies and private companies. Without satellites, astronauts would never have orbited the Earth and they would never have landed on the Moon.

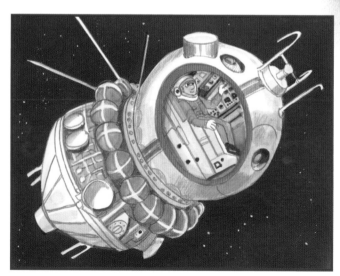

THE FIRST CREWED SPACECRAFT, Vostok 1, made one orbit of Earth. It proved that it was possible for people to go into space and return safely.

THE INTERNATIONAL SPACE STATION is the biggest Earth satellite ever. It's as if a football field were orbiting Earth about 250 miles (400 km) above the ground.

Top Tip

The International Space Station is so big that you can see it in the night sky. It looks like a bright star. Visit https://spotthestation.nasa.gov/sightings. Type in your town to find out when you can see it.

EIGHT APOLLO spacecraft orbited the Moon as lunar satellites. Six of these missions landed a total of 12 astronauts on the Moon.

RUSSIAN SOYUZ SPACECRAFT have been carrying people to Earth orbit since the 1960s. Today, they carry people and supplies to the International Space Station.

What's on TV?

We're used to seeing events all over the world on our television screens just as they are happening. We can watch the Olympic Games live, wherever they're being held. We can watch important news events as they occur. Satellites make this possible. They beam television pictures around the world at the speed of light. Before there were satellites to do this, film or videotapes of an event had to be put on a plane and flown to a television company, perhaps on the other side of the world, before they could appear on television a day or two later.

TELEVISION TRUCKS with satellite dishes on top let reporters broadcast live pictures of an event to television screens anywhere in the world.

Reporting live from the scene!

A television broadcaster sends programs up to a satellite in orbit. The satellite receives the programs and then retransmits them back down to Earth. The satellite can broadcast to a vast area of the ground.

TELEVISION SATELLITES are as big as a bus, and they're covered with lots of aerials and dishes for sending and receiving radio signals.

SOME TELEVISION SATELLITES broadcast programs directly to people's homes. The signal from the satellite is picked up by a small dish on the side of the house.

I think the satellite's out that way.

19

Keeping Track

When scientists want to know where wild animals live, where they hunt for food, or where they spend the winter months, they attach radio transmitters to the animals. Then the animals are tracked by scientists following the radio signals. Some animals are tracked on foot or by car, but those that travel great distances are tracked by satellite. Vehicles and people can be fitted with satellite tags, too, and tracked in the same way. If satellite tracking couldn't be done, lots of animal behavior would still be a mystery.

SEA CREATURES can be fitted with satellite tags that fall off after a while. The tags pop up to the surface of the water and send information stored in their memory to a satellite.

THIS LEOPARD has been put to sleep for a few minutes by a tranquilizer dart so that a satellite tracking collar can be fitted around its neck.

Don't make it too tight!

He's ready to go!

How It Works

A tiny GPS receiver in a satellite tag or collar figures out its own location and passes this information to a radio transmitter. The transmitter sends it up to a satellite, which beams it to wildlife researchers on the ground.

TAGGING EAGLES tells scientists about where the birds nest and where they hunt for food. It can also reveal where creatures eaten by the eagles are most plentiful.

SATELLITE TAGGING showed that some of the killer whales living in the freezing waters around Antarctica migrate all the way to the tropics and back.

The Business of Space

ots of businesses rely on satellites for communication as well as for accurate timing. Big businesses have computers and other equipment that all have their own internal clocks. It is important that all the clocks in different buildings, cities, and countries tell the same time. This is accomplished by using the superaccurate atomic clocks in satellites to correct errors in clocks on the ground. Power, manufacturing, and banking all depend on precise timing provided by satellites. If there were no satellites, these businesses would have to find other ways of working together.

THE OIL INDUSTRY is a big user of satellites. Satellite pictures are used in the search for oil. Satellites also ensure that drilling rigs are put in exactly the right positions.

THE WORLDWIDE BANKING SYSTEM relies on satellites for communication and providing accurate timing for millions of movements of cash around the world every day.

POWER COMPANIES have to supply as much electricity as their customers need. Information from weather satellites helps them to figure out how much electricity they will have to produce.

You Can Do It!

Put two clocks side by side and set them to the same time. Check them every day. How long is it before they show different times? Businesses use satellites to correct their clocks and stop them from drifting apart like this.

LARGE NETWORKS like the Internet, cell phones, and cable television use satellites to link different parts of their networks and make sure that they work together seamlessly.

Space Telescopes

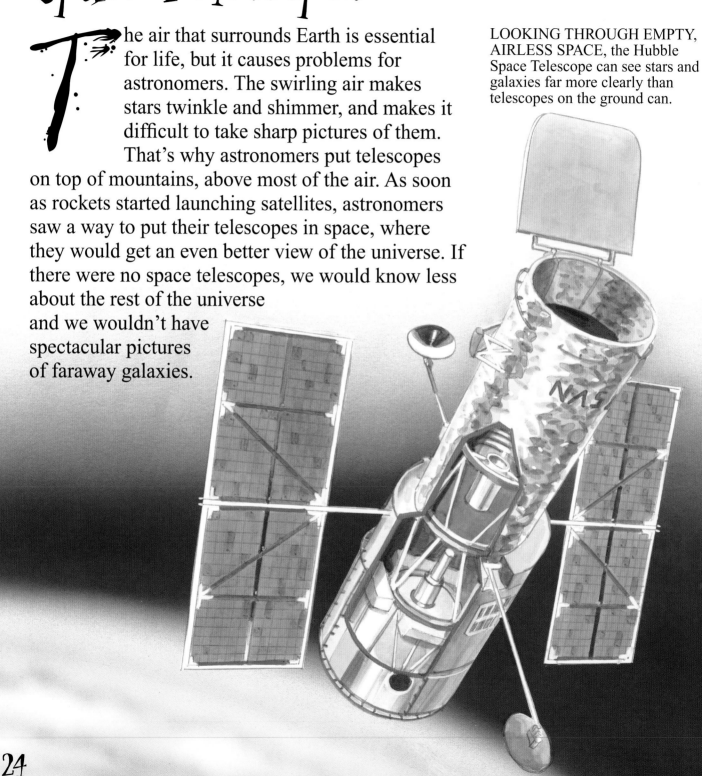

The air that surrounds Earth is essential for life, but it causes problems for astronomers. The swirling air makes stars twinkle and shimmer, and makes it difficult to take sharp pictures of them. That's why astronomers put telescopes on top of mountains, above most of the air. As soon as rockets started launching satellites, astronomers saw a way to put their telescopes in space, where they would get an even better view of the universe. If there were no space telescopes, we would know less about the rest of the universe and we wouldn't have spectacular pictures of faraway galaxies.

LOOKING THROUGH EMPTY, AIRLESS SPACE, the Hubble Space Telescope can see stars and galaxies far more clearly than telescopes on the ground can.

If you look at stars after dark, you can see why telescopes are put in space. Stars twinkle because light from them bends this way and that as it travels through the air. Viewed from space, stars do not twinkle, and so pictures of them are sharper.

It's all a blur.

Twinkle, twinkle little star.

BEFORE TELESCOPES could be put in space, astronomers had to settle for a blurry view of the stars through the atmosphere.

SOME ENERGY WAVES from space, including X-rays, can't get through the atmosphere. They can be studied only by telescopes in space. The XMM Newton is an X-ray telescope.

THE WISE TELESCOPE was launched to study infrared energy waves in space. It found thousands of comets and asteroids that had never been seen before.

Circling Other Planets

THE ROSETTA SPACECRAFT stayed with a comet called 67P/Churyumov-Gerasimenko for three years. It ended its mission in 2016 by landing on the comet.

Most satellites orbit Earth, but some spacecraft are satellites of other planets. One became a satellite of a comet. Another orbited an asteroid. Others have orbited the Moon. These spacecraft often spend years circling other worlds and studying them up close with their cameras and scientific instruments. They have spotted storms, lightning, and volcanoes on faraway planets and moons. If these spacecraft had not been sent across the solar system to orbit other worlds, we wouldn't know much about Jupiter's colorful atmosphere, Saturn's rings, superfast winds on Neptune, or the fascinating moons that orbit Jupiter and Saturn.

WOW!

These are the latest from Cassini.

THE CASSINI SPACECRAFT orbited Saturn, studying the ringed planet and its moons for 13 years, until it was commanded to end its mission by diving into Saturn's atmosphere in 2017.

THE EXOMARS
TRACE GAS ORBITER
is designed to "sniff" the
Martian atmosphere as it
orbits the planet looking
for gases that might have
been produced by life.

The satellites that orbit other
planets from Mercury to Jupiter
use solar panels to make electricity
from sunlight. Beyond Jupiter,
satellites are nuclear powered.

THE LUNAR
RECONNAISSANCE ORBITER
was placed in orbit around the
Moon to make a detailed map of
its surface to prepare for future
manned landings.

THE NEAR SHOEMAKER
spacecraft became a satellite of
an asteroid called 433 Eros. It
orbited the asteroid for a year
before ending its mission by
landing on it, like Rosetta.

Space Junk

Have you ever wondered what happens to all the old satellites that don't work any more and the rockets that put them in space? Many of them are still in orbit. Some drift through space and crash into each other or explode, sending clouds of junk flying in all directions. Bits of old space vehicles travel so fast that they can damage new satellites. If the problem of space junk isn't solved, and if it's allowed to get worse, we might have to learn to do without satellites again. Can you imagine a future without satellites?

PARTS OF OLD ROCKETS stranded in space still have some fuel left inside. If they are hit by another piece of junk, the fuel sometimes explodes.

THE INTERNATIONAL SPACE STATION has to be moved several times a year to avoid pieces of space junk.

Phew, that was close!

AFTER DECADES of launching satellites, Earth is surrounded by millions of pieces of space junk. Space agencies track thousands of the larger pieces.

How It Works

To avoid creating new space junk, satellites that are no longer working are now moved away from busy satellite orbits, and rockets dump their fuel so that they can't explode. This is called passivation.

Graveyard orbit →

SPACE JUNK often falls back to Earth. Most of it burns up in the atmosphere, but large pieces sometimes survive their fall and land on the ground.

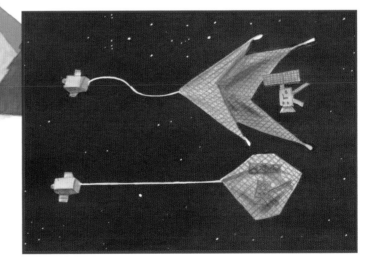

ONE IDEA for solving the space junk problem is to catch old rockets and satellites in nets and tow them back down into the atmosphere to burn up or land safely in the ocean.

Glossary

Asteroid One of the millions of rocky objects that orbit the Sun. Smaller than planets, they are also called minor planets or planetoids.

Astronomer A scientist who studies space, planets, moons, stars, galaxies, and the rest of the universe.

Atmosphere The gases that surround the Earth or another planet, or moon.

Atomic clock An extremely accurate type of clock that measures the passage of time by counting the natural vibrations of atoms.

Climate The weather in one place over a long period of time.

Comet An object made of ice and rock that orbits the Sun. When it nears the Sun, some of the ice changes to gas, sending dust flying off the comet to form a bright tail.

Decade Ten years.

Equator An imaginary line around the middle of a planet, equally distant from the poles.

Galaxies Millions or billions of stars traveling through space with clouds of gas and dust, held together by gravity. Our solar system belongs to a galaxy called the Milky Way.

Glacier A river of ice that slowly flows downhill.

Horizon An imaginary line in the distance, where the sky and Earth's surface seem to meet.

Multistage rocket A rocket made of two or more parts called stages that each has its own fuel and at least one rocket motor.

Navigation Planning a route from one place to another.

Orbit The path of one object as it travels around another object while the two are held together by gravity, such as the path of a satellite as it travels around Earth.

Radiation belts Regions of space around Earth where there are lots of electrically charged particles.

Receiver A device that detects, or receives, radio signals.

Rocket A vehicle, usually tube-shaped, that climbs to a great height and continues to work in space. Rockets launch satellites and other spacecraft.

Satellite A natural or artificial object that orbits another body in space. The Moon is a natural satellite of Earth. The International Space Station is an example of an artificial satellite of Earth.

Satellite tag A small device that can be attached to an animal, person, or machine to transmit its location and other information up to a satellite in space.

Solar panel A sheet of solar cells that take in sunlight and convert it into electric current.

Solar system The Sun and all the planets, moons, and other objects that travel through space with it.

Space Shuttle One of several reusable crewed spacecraft that made repeated journeys between Earth and space between 1981 and 2011.

Space station A large spacecraft that stays in space for years and is visited by a series of astronaut crews.

Space telescope An astronomical instrument launched into space, where it can see the rest of the universe without being affected by Earth's atmosphere.

Space vehicle Another name for a spacecraft.

Transmitter A type of device that sends out, or transmits, radio signals.

Universe Everything that exists everywhere.

Index

Top Satellite Pioneers

Konstantin Tsiolkovsky (1857–1935)
Tsiolkovsky was a schoolteacher in Russia who studied rockets and spaceflight in the 1890s. He came up with the idea of a multistage rocket and figured out how fast a rocket had to go to put a spacecraft in orbit. Engineers and inventors in other countries read about his ideas and went on to build and launch the first space rockets.

Robert H. Goddard (1882–1945)
In 1926, Goddard launched the first rocket that burned liquid fuel. It was a vital step in the development of rockets for launching satellites. The power of a liquid-fueled rocket can be varied by sending more fuel or less fuel to the rocket motor. The motor can even be turned off and fired again later. Goddard launched more than 30 rockets. Some of his inventions are still used in rockets today. NASA's Goddard Space Flight Center was named after him.

Arthur C. Clarke (1917–2008)
In 1945, British science-fiction writer Arthur C. Clarke wrote a magazine article about using satellites for communication. He said that a satellite 22,300 miles (36,000 km) above Earth would stay over the same spot on the ground, and that only three of these satellites would be needed to send radio signals between any two places on Earth.

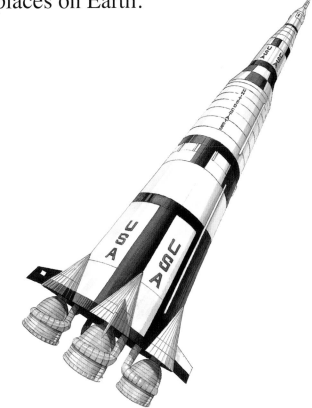

The Future of Satellites

In the future, satellites may communicate in a new way. Today they use radio, but light beams can carry far more information. Future satellites may communicate with light instead of radio. In 2013, a spacecraft orbiting the Moon successfully communicated with its controllers on Earth by light.

The first satellites were small. Sputnik 1 was a small ball only 23 inches (58 centimeters) across.

Later satellites were bigger, some as big as a bus. But these satellites can take years to build and cost millions of dollars to launch. While these big satellites will still be used in the future, there will also be more "smallsats." These smaller satellites, also called microsatellites and nanosatellites, cost a great deal less to construct and launch.

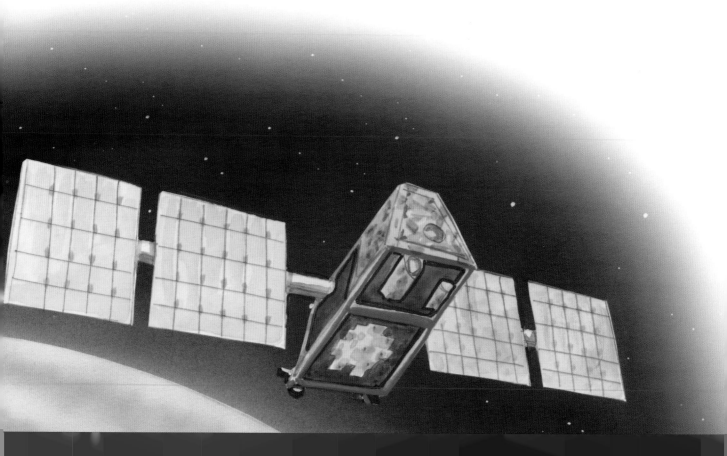

Did You Know?

An American telephone satellite and a Russian military communications satellite crashed into each other by accident on February 10, 2009. Both satellites were destroyed. It was the first serious satellite crash.

NASA's first space station, Skylab, fell to Earth in 1979. When parts of it landed on the southeast coast of Western Australia, the town of Esperance fined NASA $400 for littering! In 2009, a California radio show host raised money from his listeners and paid the fine.

Several faulty satellites have been repaired in space by astronauts. In 1992, astronauts repaired a communications satellite that had gotten stuck in the wrong orbit. In 1993, the Hubble Space Telescope had to be repaired by astronauts. In 1984, two communications satellites in the wrong orbit were brought back to Earth by the Space Shuttle. Both satellites were launched again successfully in 1990.

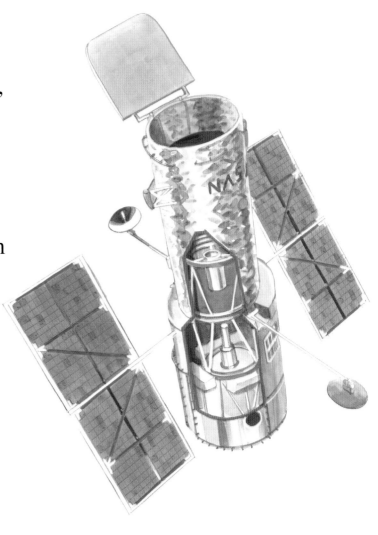